ALEgRÍA

PUBLISHING

wisdom *looks* good on *her*

wisdom *looks* good on *her*

Monica Salazar

ALE*g*RÍA

PUBLISHING

PUBLISHING

Wisdom Looks Good on Her
© 2024 Monica Salazar
ISBN: 9798991125031

First Edition, 2024

Printed in the United States of America

Edited by Caroline Depalma
Front Cover Photograph by Brianna Lee
Cover Design by Kim Gaeta Brown
Layout Design by Jim Dodson
Book cover photo by Brianna Lee Anguiano

To

God, who's given me all my blessings
My mother who taught me love and divine love
My father who who taught me about self-love and the love of art
My Tia who infused the love of writing and magic
My friends who are family for their undying love and support
My family who reminds me to never give up and keep living my dream

To *Julian Salazar*
To *Uncle Joe*
To *Sammy Salazar*
To *my grandparents*
To *my ancestors, guides and angels*

this ones for you

Thank you Hiram Sims
& my double one familia

Contents

Forward from Mama

Monica,

My dearest youngest daughter, I want you to have this lovely delicately designed journal in honor of of your eight grade graduation. I hope you will be loyal and dedicated to journal writing. Don't write because you have to, but write because you want to. something good for *you*!

If you pray and ask the Holy Spirit to inspire and guide you, you'll always have something to spill out on paper. Write about what you love, what you hate. Write about your hopes and dreams scribble down crazy thoughts and sagacious ones. Make up a prayer now and then. Whatever you do, don't be afraid to write

write, write.

Love from Mom

ps one day I'll see your writing published. I really believe in you.

Chapter 1

wisdom of self-*love*

The Gravity of Me

I am always fascinated by the people who just create their life
Their example gets me out of victim mode
Shows me how the human spirit works
How their insides reflect their outside

A magnetic pull

Like moth to
a flame typa energy
Like I've come
this far typa energy
I don't give
a fuck typa energy

So I rise, wash the weight of dark away

The in-between of me and her
The spacey worn out place where we stand
Solid ground?
Not so sure
Where I am at, beginning to clear

Here I am again, moving through space
Choosing which pain
As I sift through a rock and hard place
To meet my highest self
Earth is preparation
To levels of consciousness

A war within, to conquer the spirit of sin
But
Sin is just a misstep, a space that needs more light
The dark place where all the lessons are learned
And boy, do I love learning

The world a mirror that I learn to see from the inside out
How do we get through a day with all this chaos?
The earth turning over from the ground under
Jolted awake to see children dying everyday
I cross my hand from my head to my heart as I let my tears fall
They remind me of my aliveness, my blessings that nourish me

Take away my identity and on bended knee
I am just me
Always aching to stay awake
Choosing momentary pain over suffering
I look to the heavens and say
I think I can do this again
Like my ancestors before me
For I hear them say,
   "rise again"

Despite it all
Despite not being born a certain way
Into a certain body
Into a certain time and place
Character development they call it

This is the gravity of me
This is my story
Layers and layers, pages and pages
Not just one thing

Made up of countless conversations, heartaches, wins and losses
Wisdom looks good on me
      I see, I see
So this is what being a light bearer means
Surrendering to the flames

Remembering My Own Height

This is the year I am excited to meet her
The dismantling of my new beginning
This year I meet the love of my life
For she grew up with what it felt like
Disney movies the hope that sprung from the little lies that love is on the outside

So this is the year where I ignore his height and remember my own
This is the year where I choose the discomfort of nerves instead of the comfort of fear that keeps me safe

This is the year where I stay focused on attending that negative feeling transmuting it into some sort of meaning

This is the year were the sun, eclipses, full moons, guide me back to my path

This is the year where I dive into the dark parts of me that need to stay alive to bring earth to the skies. This is a year where change needs me, desires me, feeds me, craves me into loving existence

This is the year where I will be open to love. I won't say no to love. I'll just recognize when I see it or when I don't.

Rocket Ships

Rock bottom it's where you find yourself again
It is where writing becomes rewriting
It is where you delve within to find your superpower
Becoming a little more divine
Rocks become rocket ships

As you look to your
Inner compass, a new world

That reflects all that you are

Be who you are who you will be
all and nothing, up and down
whole and empty all at once.
all together you make up the
the stars that created you
and the earth that formed you
a combination of both ocean
and sand with the warmth of
the sun and fullness of the moon
what richness it is to know you
the witness to the changing tides
what an honor it is

Start From Scratch

Sometimes it feels like you're losing all your powers
The little magical parts of you that make you,you.

The spark

When it starts to fade

                    you think

Well maybe it's just a bad day
Or my period is about to start
Or maybe I need a good cry

Or maybe I will just start from scratch, again

I get to focus on me
and what i found was
a gaint
        a goddess
                a warrior
who was love all along
who believed in her
    all along

my only regret was

staying long - to convince
    you -

Alter

What I embody
does not lie in need
this is beyond desire
the infinite that challenges the soul

What I offer
a table of plenty
I am the altar

The offering of the deepest truths
in the deepest shadows as
the strongest light

The oracle, the chosen one
yet humbling myself to ash
Dying to my ego
just to raise the divine
birthing all possibilities

to claim the notion that
presence is my power
to sit all my everything and
nothing
all my empty and
all my vastness

Just show up
See what magic
 Flows to you
     Breathe in and out

  Narrow in. XXXX Slowly...
in the moment, sink...

    blood goes where the energy flows
 Awake...deep sigh...let me show you
  Love.
 What it smells like,
 What it tastes like,
   What it breathes like
 Let it take you under
     that sweet spot
  hold it sweetly
 For it a force more powerful

  than our bodies combined
 Something Divine

Romántica

Be a poet, but keep the romance to myself
For I have been adorned by roses from behind the veil
As water drips from my hips
Just to let you float in pools of serenity
Integrate me and you will live beyond time and space

Be a poet, but give the romance to those who see me, fully
Like how I see you, unapologetically naked
As my poems quench your thirst to be seen
My words, sage for the suffering
Soften hard water into oasis, endless vacations

Be a poet, see my world through rose hues
On rainy days we stay in bed, make love
Drink cacao like our ancestors did
Let the sun bring melanin to our skin again

Be a poet, apart of my world
Where I will scribble about you on scraps of paper
Just to novel you into the history books, about our love
Because life with a poet
goes on to live forever

Be a poet, for others
But most importantly
Be a poet for myself

Bookkeeper of My Heart

Is a place I go where unwritten words bloom
in shadowy spaces
Of untangled thoughts that act
careless, wild, free
Rooted amongst the chaos is a little girl that
I'm meeting for the first time, again
I sit and read about her mystery
endless magic and wonder
about the world that spirals
into soulful insights endless pages
revealing her inner secrets and desires
of her untamed, bandaged, beautiful heart
I'm in love with her and
I've been in love with her my whole life and

I didn't even know it

Holy

Have you ever dipped down into your own well of love
The one you give so freely to others
Have you felt the resistance of it?
The uncomfortability of it all?
We weren't taught to be our own love

But we are the first of many generations to come
We are the first to break curses
Break churches that told us bad was black good was white
When bad is just the dark that needs more light
Not knowing that is what makes us whole
Holy - divine and human

Brown Girl Rest

The revolution of brown girl rest
Let me take a long bath with lavender and rose petals
sink into the melody of soft piano music
Let water hold me, tender candle light melt me

Before we crave nourishment
followed by a long Sunday afternoon nap
let me take my time on this meal for you and I
Let each bite awaken you little by little
This is how I show you I care
When I take my time to make something just right

Let me sit and read this book
Read it out loud until you fall asleep
So you can rest too

Let me lie awake in bed for an hour as you study me in rest
Wanna waste time? Breakfast in bed with bad rom coms
where we end up kissing too many naked parts of each other

Can we rest and forget about the world that so often forgets about us
Let me comfort to feel my nerves, the ones I numb at my 9-5
Is it really only Sunday?
Let me call off tomorrow and let's do Sunday again
because I think I am starting to remember myself again
As I surrender a little softer in my own soul and brown skin

Our life is not valued in always pleasing and serving others
Producing, productive, pouring and pouring
Do we dare to love ourselves to love each other better?
In community or in partnership
Reminders like this, make living less lonely, less tiring

Brown girl, yellow, black, and all the hues

Rest.

Call this rebellious,
As we listen to our bodies
that rises with the moon and moves with the tides
Call this revolutionary,
The act of calming our nervous system
we so tirelessly burn.

Valley girls are the prettiest

away from the city influence
smog and dust dont cloud their
      judgement
sweet as honey sour power hour

where time kisses her skin in slow
      motion
worry free, full of dreams

held by real ones
the ones who have known her   *

through thick n thin

trend setter with any weather

dont forget about family, home

thats where she goes
when left alone

from granada hills to valley village

valley girls there is no one like
em - no love like theirs.

Devastatingly Deserving

There are flowers next to my bed
not because I am sick
but because I am worthy

He brings me flowers after the others pass away
served their time next to mine, for you see,
To open the heart of every femme - they need flowers
from him or ones she buys or picks herself

No reason, no occasion needed
just to say, "I care about you."
I appreciate you existing in this world
standing tall in bloom
just to unearth you after rainfall

There are flowers next to my bed
they tell me I am devisingly deserving
As I drift off to sleep
they dance in the night sky making wishes for me

I awaken to starlit yellow roses and white baby's breath
They grant me permission
to be awed and adored

Speak to me with flowers, no occasion or reason
But just to remind me that I too
deserve to be celebrated in every season I breathe breath

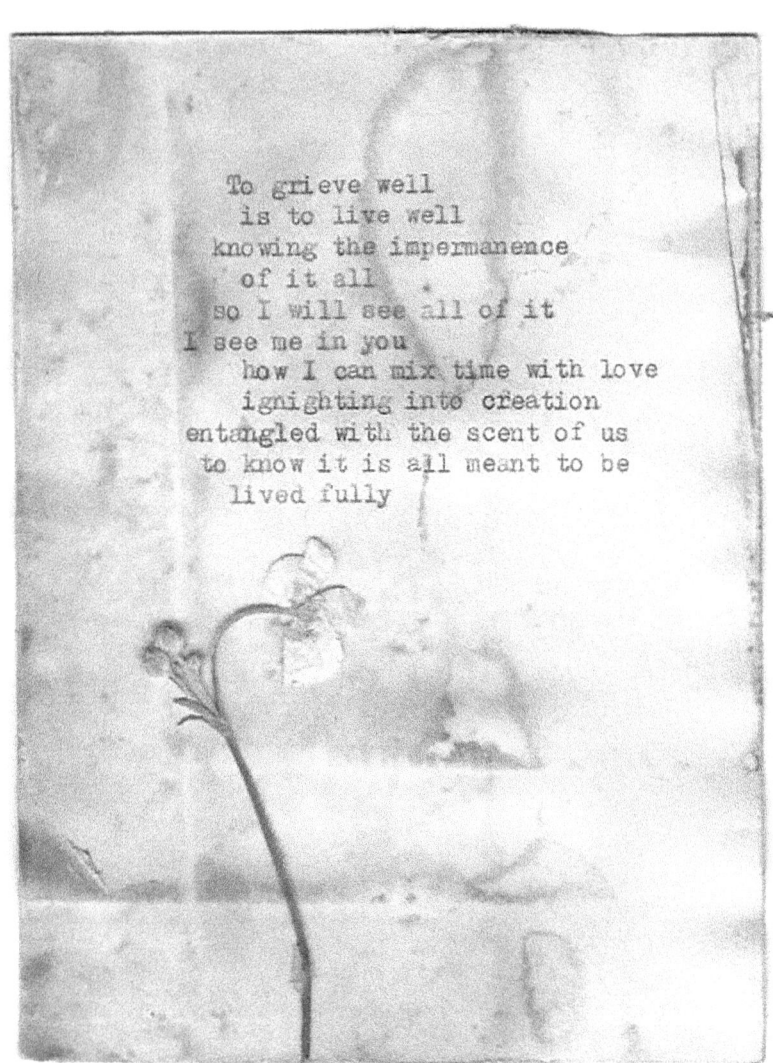

To grieve well
   is to live well
 knowing the impermanence
   of it all
 so I will see all of it
I see me in you
     how I can mix time with love
     ignighting into creation
 entangled with the scent of us
 to know it is all meant to be
    lived fully

The Year of Remembering

This is the year of surrender,
Where the tired unwanted layers fadeaway
Where my ideas materialize

come to life

This is the year
Where we walk hand in hand with the unknown
Where action takes place when I don't feel like it
Where we walk a little wiser, break concrete patterns
Like the ones my grandma would find freeing
Where we release the boys who play god
The men who play boys, and
The exes who still want to be friends

This is the year
I discover what it means to truly love
expansively, relentlessly
But most importantly, authentically

But wait,
If I say I am
I am love, I am abundant
Will I be tested?
Will I allow myself to be
Goddesses strongest warrior
Romanticize the shit outta everything chaotic
Just to craft into something harmonious
like a good poet

This is the year I will allow myself to be fully seen
Allow myself to believe good things happen to me

So this is the year where I will have
Morning routines, drink rose tea, smoke lavender, drip drops of honey
To fill my cup, and
move accordingly into my becoming
And never forget, that my dreams that are dreaming me back

Chapter 2

wisdom of *family*

Abuelita Monaquita

My mouth naturally curves downward
My lips resemble the mouth of my father's mother
Mi Abuelita

I can't help but wonder if hers grew more downward since her birth
I can't help but wonder if her upside down smile
grew more from the pain he would break on her skin
From brown to blue
From a man who said he loved her

She stayed silent in grace
As she met uncertainty with faith
How she maintained the pain that makes me wonder
What I inherited

Does pain mean love? Does love mean pain?
Two extremes
Am I meant to speak out against it
Speak out what she so silently endured
From a man who stayed but did not love her

So I curve my mouth upwards towards the sky
To the sun to dry her tired eyes
To tell her story in a new light
Her prayers were not in vain
How she past down her pain
But also her strength and resilience

The magic she carried as she prayed on each rosary bead
Traveled to my mouth to speak out
About the warm love she gave
To transcend black and blue
So that I get to choose
So I turn my frown upside down
As she made me smile when she named me Monaquita, Moniquita
Little Monica, Little doll
The one who will change it all
I will always remember your warm magic
I will always speak out for you too

Mama's Prayer

Jesus Mercy Mary Joseph
Mama had to call on all whole damn divine family
When something went wrong
Or when stress was high - like all the time
All these kids, don't know what to do with
But I'd give anything to hear her say that again
How she maintained and mismanaged the chaos

A magic I did not know existed
As you held love that turned into black and white thinking
Jesus Mercy Mary Help Us
.
The baby to 7 siblings
What was the point of it all in the end?
As you left us with all our 8 sins
But I was left with the best version of you

Baby, you were set from the beginning
With all the good love no boundaries
No strict rules set for me
Like the ones who suffered before me
Jesus Mercy Mary Help Them

What was that for?
I know I came here to spark love into you
Your desire to do it right again
Was my desire too, to give and receive
But you left before I could say "I do"

Jesus Mercy Mary and Joseph
The whole damn divine family
I'm sure you met them by now
And they chuckled for they knew you
I'm not sure if I should lean on them too
For I believe my god is from above and within
But I still believe in their union
How I wish it for our family too
In times of stress I pray
Jesus Mercy Mary Joseph help me too

You Are So Beautiful

I don't know how to tell you this
but, You are so beautiful
Like how my grandma used to say
Her memory was lost on her
But she had eyes for remembering

as she stared into my face
a familiar landscape
Like star gazing but picking out the
parts that mirrored her

I remind her who I am, *I'm Monica, your grand-daughter.*
The comfort in her awe struck eyes
as she says
"You're so beautiful"
I am gifted with
Meeting her first time reactions
Every time

I don't think I was much to look at
untamed hair, sunken eyes
I knew mom praised my smile
my father said "you're so cute, my littlest doll"

But my grandma
with forgotten memory
Said, *Beautiful*

the weight of this word
carried majesty
And responsibility

I began to believe her
every time I reintroduced myself
Staring into the depths of my eyes
speaking into well of my soul
In a spark of remembrance she reminds me

"You are so beautiful"

Sweet Wild Boys

These are my nephews. I've changed their diapers and babysat them
with my mother in a house filled with crevices in need of exploring.
They managed to explore every inch of that old house. The place is
filled with memories, music, magic, mamá, make believe, make-ups,
mischief, madness. Freedom.
Madness and freedom.

I got to delight in their wild and abrupt eagerness, rampaging around
the land that seemed to be their kingdom.

Inside, the matriarch was reading, praying, making or resting. Wishing
maybe they would cuddle up and read the Bible with her, create some-
thing or sit and eat. They didn't eat too much.
Their food was cake or worms.

Boys,

a quest for aimless power in a silly gust of wind that ferociously invigo-
rates their spirit and heart. As they grasp the fleeting moments of what it
means to be a boy.
That's how I would describe my observation and admiration of them.
My sweet, wild boys.

Papa Bear

"Papa is a bear in hibernation.
That's why he snores," mama said
I sneak under the covers
I am part bear
I bury my nose in her chest
It is furry and soft like blanket

She smells of honey and blueberries that
She picked by the stream for me to eat
While papa bear hunted for meat
Raw fish drizzled with lemon

We are well fed brown bears
After we will play in the streams,
Let our fur dry in the sunbeams
Chase butterflies and climb trees

Night falls and I lay near my brother who sleeps silently
A nightmare wakes me and the cave is dark and moody
I whimper for mama and papa to comfort me
Nowhere to be seen, I jolt my brother awake to walk me to their den
He does not fight me as he yawns and wanders sleepily through the
night crawl
Until I am met with the melody of snores

Mama gently pulls me in close to her warm and beating heart
The streams of the river shush me to sleep again
Dreams of honey dripped lips and blueberries paws fill my mind

"Grrrrr" I am awakened from my sleep again
As I see papa rise early for work
I giggle to the sound of his snarls and grunts
As I am tickled by the strongest paws I have ever felt

Mama's Masterpiece

This is a love letter - not the one where he wins my heart and things get better
It's for the girl born in 1947
The woman married in 1972
The woman who dedicated her life to "I love you's" and "Pray don't worry baby things will be alright."

A woman so much apart of my life if I told you she broke my heart you'd swear I was lying
But she didn't mean to, she did mean to leave
She didn't mean to leave a church so full it felt so god damn empty without her
She didn't mean to stop making more memories for us to hold on to
She didn't mean to leave her baby girl at 25 to figure it out all out on her own
But She meant to be vibrant and full choosing to love every second of her life

Mama,
You spoke your mind about what's wrong and right
You stood your ground and walked so strong with hips fearlessly sway-ing side to side
Yet all the while your smile so bright
Your wit so charged it turned on lights
Your body spoke the language of love
Carrying babies, craving hugs
Your mind never left you, your heart never stopped you and your spirit is still you
Yet your body failed.

But I forgive you for leaving so soon.
Left with a wound so full and deep that will one day heal
But just like love and for love it will always remain.
This is a love letter for the girl who looks like her mother
At 28 too scared to say goodbye she instead embodies her
In the way she talks,
the way she walks
In the way she sways and in the way she loves
Because you promised you'd always be with me
I'll be your masterpiece in the making.
You be the artist.

Whose Shoulders Do You Stand On?

Mama was arrested
Handcuffed in the back of a cop car
Next to the Chicano House on the Northridge campus
That burnt down on Cinco de Mayo

Just the night before it was home to
Collective gatherings where thought leaders discussed
Freedom around food, music and laughter
Brown warmth, fed, loved community home
Was now a pile of ash and rubble

I can see her now walking the burnt down grounds
Probably yelling and cursing into the air of what remained

In my time - a hate crime
In my time - intense investigation
In my time - boycotts, riots, protests
In her time - just an accident
In her time - nothing to see here
In her time - too scared to speak up

But she did
Handcuffed for involving herself with her friends arrest
At the fallen Chicano Casita
She never told me this story of what it felt like to be mistreated by the cops

Did she put up a fight?
Did she comply?
Did she get angry like me, break down and cry?

My mother said "we were just so angry back then - we made the mistake of not praying before marching or protesting…"
Si mama pero - the sound of my father's guitar and his mariachi band were prayers no?
They say when you sing you pray twice
She clutches her rosary beads and says, yes but if you don't have god…
I can't remember the rest
But she wanted to the forget the past

Maybe it hurt too much
She instead lifted her life in prayer, raising children and kissing the cook

Part 2. Whose Shoulders Do You Stand On?

My father - 1st generation Mexican, noticed my mother's laugh at that
Chicano House
Bound for trade school my father never thought college was for him until
a high school teacher said:
"You know Gilbert, you're smart. You don't have to go to trade school,
you can make into to college."

This small moment changed his trajectory
The boy raised in Mexicali, musically gifted, loved to cook
Walked to school with this brother on dirt roads
Worked during summers picking peaches on the farm
While Mama was probably picking out new shoes

He regretting playing football like his older brother
And wish he played in the school band
But somehow found his way back to the strings of the guitar
Followed by her laugh as the melody and his heart as the beat

The Mexican American Princess (M.A.P.), who was a laugh a minute
Life of the party, 3rd generation, pretty, light skinned girl
Was taken by the the soft-spoken, loyal mariachi boy who only had eyes
for her

She was ambitious as the oldest of 8 children
She was set out to set the example
Woman of the year at her college
Only had tea while the other girls had ice cream

Was told she was a fox as she rolled her eyes at players
She was looking for someone special who only had eyes for her

His name was Gilbert
Her name was Monica

She brought the light and laughter
As he was lifted from the long walks on dusty roads
And hot summer fruit fields

He brought her back to her deepest roots of her identity and calm
serenity
Back to the shoulders of her ancestry
Their love kindled into an ever burning flame
Ever rebuilding like the rising walls of the Chicano Casita

This is was the beginning of my history and the shoulders I stand on

Comfort

Hola Mija, how are you?

Are the most comforting words a brown girl can hear

Gracias, Tia, Tios and Grandparents

My Sisters Hands

My little legs dangle on the fur covered porcelain thrown
I sit straddled facing the blue bathroom wall
I am instructed to
not move my head
I sigh and ask
"Are we done yet?"

"Yes!" My sister says
just 5 more minutes
but I don't mind
because I am with her
and she is styling my hair

My thick brown hair
My crown I did not care too much for
or the weight it would eventually carry
For now, my sister brushes it for nice occasions - her job, not mine

My hair, the one I run hose water through on hot summer days
From running too much as sun melts through me
My hair, the one that has a weird hairline
so we put bangs on it

My sister says, "why can't I find a perfect part line"
Yet she folds my hair to one side
uncovers a perfect line
amongst the weeds and tangles
a path to my pretty, to the lineage where I will
one day part off on my own
And remember how to use hands that will braid tails my own

I sigh but not to rush the master
my sisters hands
As they weave in and out
all around
pull and tug, careful not to say ouch
hot iron smell, burnt hair
Moose sticks to my forehead

I wonder what's going on up there
But I know, my sisters hands are meant for
making things look pretty
because mama is too tired, too busy

I love my sisters hands
That holds the weight of my hair
as she says almost done
But I don't mind because
I am with her
and soon I will look pretty as a princess
Pretty like her crown of hair

Mariachi Daughter

El Rey blares through the car windows
I join in with Chente,
"No tengo trona no reina
Ni nadie que me comprenda
Pero sigo siendo el Rey"

Something about not having a thrown or queen
or someone understanding
but I am still King
My Spanish fails me
Wasn't taught it growing up as a 4th generation
Mexican-American

But I am still my father's daughter in this way
A Mariachi's Daughter
Met with memories of my father practicing
on the violin or singing with the guitar
To be worthy of wearing the charro suit

His black fitted suit was with interwoven silver ornaments and buckles
That climb on the side of the trousers and
His short jacket was adorned with charms too
a silver roster buckled at the front
He completed his attire with
cowboy boots and a red, wide bow tie laced with gold
Worn with elegance and pride

He combs his hair to one side and sprays his best cologne
Saturday night gig with his compadres where he would sing
to swooning abuelitas
or be background music at an anniversary party somewhere in LA
Still, the magic of the band was in need

I would ask him to translate rancheros to me
how alarming heartbreaking they would be
Or how they'd make me fall in love with love again

My father loved mama like that
the typa love that could only be from a Mariachi
The romantic yet still strong masculine man

They don't make them like that anymore

Always with passion
The heart of a Mariachi is either weeping
or madly in love - no in between it seems
and if they are - they're not living
The ballads of a bleeding Mexican heart
How we yearn, how we long
how we love

Something familiar in me when love comes along
As Vincente sings
"Las horas mas hermosas de mi vida, Las he pasado al lado
de una dama."
how I could be that Mujeres Divina
the most beautiful hours of someone's life
would be the time they've spent with me
and they would sing about it

I sigh and wonder
Does the universe still make them like they used too?

The curse of being a Mariachi's daughter

The Assembly Line

It's a siblings birthday and they want
Enchiladas for dinner
But this is no one man's job

The grated cheese with finely chopped
onions and olives
the spicy enchilada sauce and
the tortillas that need frying
are waiting for us on the counter

It is my job to scope the cheese mixture
into the fried tortillas dipped in sauce
fold them up and start on the next one
until the baking sheet was filled to the brim

I don't dare touch the job of frying tortillas
hot oil jumps from the pan kisses my skin like a sting
So one of my brothers handles it

These are dads instructions
I am not sure if we couldn't wait to finish while
fixing a birthday dinner or enjoyed the time creating together
but it's simply just a memory worth
remembering
our assembly line was
all about working together
seamlessly, collaboratively
and no bickering
All hands in, cheese, hot oil, and red sauce

I knew we all couldn't wait to eat
Bellies full with enchiladas, cake and icecream
All 8 of us in a room
Blessed to know another birthday with the same assembly line
will come again in a month or two

Breakfast with Bocelli

Mom listened to Andrea Bocelli in the mornings
before school I would walk into the kitchen to the sound
of his voice
Breakfast would be served -
My brother and I ate
while the blind opera sang to us

She felt closer to god this way
like heaven's gates were opening
just as my eyes were
It was the first time I heard the song
Solamente una Vez
that wasn't a mariachi version

Spanish guitar and weeping violin
carried his voice to my mother's spirit
as she tried to hum along
but she was tone deaf
couldn't not carry a note to save her life

But for the first time, I saw mama less busy
with less kids
falling in love with romance again
as she would say,
*"This is the day the lords has made
Let us rejoice and be glad in it!"*

She was finding happiness again
Listening to Andrea Bocelli at the break of day
with coffee and toast and cooking
for two tired teenagers,
her babies

she was falling in love
with music again
Not through papa but

with her own soul
with her own spirit
with her own serenity

Chapter 3

wisdom of *love*
& heart*break*

love notes in my brain

i cant really explain

ive made break throughs
been through lulls

highs and lows that all been safe

hardest time feeling because my
body has a hard time believing me
believing that I am safe so it
closes me off puts up walls
the viel becomes thicker
i wait for an answer
But I know this life takes me
deeper into places I dont like
or maybe just learning to love
learning to explore, what my voice
sounds like, what my body does
when its in love, do I care too much
loud or belittled by the sounds too little. Are my thoughts too
that feed the angels or the seconds
do i fight or do i face them
do i love and just embrace them

On Letting Go

I tried to see you as you are.

No judgment, no expectations

        But in your cracks and crevices

There was immense darkness I could not reach
Even my light - that drew you in - could not go there.
It would stomp me out, dim me, rob from me what I've taken so long to build.

So, I let you go.

Today I let you go - not with anger or resentment but with full peace and faith that being with you would have hurt you. Not because I would've but because you would've. I would've allowed you to walk all over me, take advantage, sacrifice myself to believe you loved me.
Not even all the love in the world couldn't fix the pain that would slowly set in.
There's something greater out there for you and maybe it's you
Loving yourself - alone - is worth it

Beginning of the End

I must be kidding myself
I might've mistaken connection for infatuation
here we go again
a chemical bliss is hard to miss

Why can I give that love back to my own body?
that spills into myself
like I am some, body to love
I know it's easier said than done
What I speak comes into existence
Which is why I believed your actions
which is why I believed your words
But you are also not me
You are simply the dust I plant my feet on
A drop in my ocean
Rising to fall

Cement

you were like cement man-made
hard as I melted my feet into you
Remember when you were
ash and bone
Dirt and mold
All the elements no one talks about
Meshed up into cement
How I thought I could make this man soft again like
Before he was made
Press my hand into the clay
Imprint love into you.
My DNA into you
Maybe mold you
Add some baby's breath
Lavender, honey
Whisper find me again
When you are cement
Let my feet recognize it's you
A foundation of strength
Make me new

I knew it wasn't love
When you left
And I found all of me

Cry Me to Sea

"I cried a river over you"
Julie London

This song reminds me of you
Cry Me a River
How you regretted your release of me
Into the the streams of uncertainty

How I would rise from the banks of the river
Just to emerge, water dripping from my hips
The god I witnessed in you
I already witnessed in me
But you saw me too late
Cry me a river

I imagined what we could be
But I am much too soft in my surrender
To fight for someone so weak
Too cowardice to love.

How all consuming it would have been
How daringly addictive with your avoidance, my anxiousness
Relentless tides to serene pools that reflect the sky
How your material stability was all I could see
But your uncertainty gave me no peace

Let my roots sink into solid ground for
I am tired of drowning
Cry me a river

I have decided to let my tears stream into
oceans of me
find myself embracing the deepest parts of me
Allowing the admiration of my waves to consume me
No longer drowning in tears of a river
but becoming the sea

Flirting With The Gods Again

His energy
Enticed her

Chemical imbalance that met her void with his and
thus began the addiction- I mean attraction
Engraving his scent with hers and her scent with his
An entanglement
With a man
Who could not love her back

When she met him she had
Endless thoughts of what could be
Future tripping
Everything will go like this
Accordingly
Days wasted daydreaming
It was 2020
She was meeting herself everyday
With clarity or thoughts of him
As she tested her power
With his uncertainty
Of how he could be
Like Prince Charming
Big strong arms
Melt in his embrace
Why him though?

While poetry ran through her veins
How her eyes sparkled with
Milky moonlight and soulful galaxies
Strawberries licked from lips that breathed life into him

But he loved cars and crypto
Hand guns and amo
To her fantasy mind
He was the modern prince
Warrior concept, masculine man she needed for her feminine
Off to battle with guns and cars
The evolution of the warrior into the modern day man
Only difference he was like talking to a caveman

Adoring eyes, she looked at him in the they way he craved
For she saw the beauty in everything
Convincing herself his feeling of safety will bring out his honor and
truth
Not knowing she was praying to a statue
A shell of a man that should just be knocked down

From the beginning of time
She would write from the inkling that turned into kindling
From bruised pain to blissful power
On rainy days with cloudy eyes
She would still write
Until she found herself in rose gardens on ray filled days

With a mind like hers
And a heart like hers
She was never going to remain
A pretty little sweet thing
As she tore open her heart
To love and risk it all
Finding things about herself she did not see at all
She was made with parts that were meant to evolve
Could not help but grow

The push and pull became exhausted
She found herself letting go
As he finalized it with a separation

She wasn't meant to stay the sweet little wild thing
The girl he imagined, wouldn't grow
Stay the same, muted everyday

With poetry in her veins
She had big dreams
Of philosophy and magic
With the history of lovers that inspired her
Like Cleopatra and Mark Anthony
Frida Khalo and Diego Rivera
Or John Lennnon and Yoko Ono
She carried this romantic idea of love
That it was a radical choice to love someone everyday

The depth of her thoughts were met with
Mysteries to solve, secrets to reveal
Because with a heart like hers
And a mind like hers
She was meant to evolve as her spirit grew into
knowing her weight in gold

Every little cell made to drink stardust and conquer death
After death
After heartbreak
Never aching for too long
Flirting with the Gods again
In all her majesty she found herself
seeing the Goddess in her

unapologetically

Angels Envy Me

I would say I'm angelic
But angel's envy me when I make love
When I dip down into touch
Soul grasps body

As Eyes roll back
Cries for the heavens to hear
As they crave for the stroke of lust
Maybe it's love in surrender
In the meeting of god's eyes
Made in his image
Skin on skin, that sensation

Breathe into your moans that hold your groans
Smelling sweet perfume as sweat drips
Electrified into deeper breaths just to
Drown into pools of
Deep brown eyes

Hands melt into tangled hair strands
Lost in passion, holding affection
When you say my name
With the timing of my cries
The swell inside,
I am reborn from flames

Yet watered over and over again
As your Fallen angel

The Muse

Every artist needs their muse
every muse their master

bodies are just skin to skin
let me, maze into you
see you how god sees you
how you see the god in you

mesmerized by the makeup of you
the labyrinth that opens Pandora's box
the grief that has a hard time feeling
the avoidance that has a hard time seeing
the stifled overflow of you that never delves too deep
Unravel all of you and somewhere there's got to be love

Why do I love like this?
Caution signs beware me
but I just snip them away
Fall into your mind the
chaos that doesn't scare me
the madness you made peace with
gives me something I know needs loving

I try not to judge my outlook or let it take me away
because studying someone at arm's length, bodies close
is how I stay safe but also entertained
I'll take notes on discoveries and observations
find it all so fascinating how you move
how being a witness to your life distracts but inspires mine too

As you find me lost in dreams
My oura reminds you
To feel again

all so collapsing,
     spiritually sanctifying

There's no mess you can't love
I see you, my master, piece
When was the last time it felt this good next to someone?
But you like resisting

that space

between you and I that persists
You suddenly remember to miss what you have yet to sink into
I don't need you to feel, what you so crave in me

Everything Is Intimate

The world is at war
And all I want to do is kiss you
In the distance ambulances are blaring
across the world children are crying

Here in this soft bed I have thoughts of us in adoration

We melted, remember?
Lost ourselves a bit there
You say kissing is very intimate
But I am a poet
So everything is intimate

But we both pull away because we're
scared to want the same thing
I like falling, but I usually end up flying anyway

I wish that children in Gaza
can grow wings
and fly
I would hold them
it would keep you off my mind

We will drive each other crazy anyway
But we would like it
Because maybe it's different,
we can create something here, like artist do I
would never get bored with you and you with me

Doesn't it sound revolutionary,
to love in a time like this?

Some days, I want to guard my heart so tightly
that I would need major convincing
like your words aligning with your actions
But some days, I am a full blown lover girl
But setting boundaries to stay this way

loving you anyway

Want to do something crazy and love like artists do?
Transcend pain into purpose

Loving on purpose
This is where dreams dance in awe of you
Imagine a new world where only love and peace reside

There is always more to it this thing called love
it is just a building block
the stone in building foundations that
won't crumble under the leadership of
mere mortal men

For you are just a mere mortal man in need of
tender-loving-care and you've gone scarce
Leave it to a woman with so much love to give
To remind us where we come from
Leave it to a woman, we will do what we do best
And no I don't mean to birthing a nation but,

Birth ideas, birth purpose, birth foundations, birth communities,
birth falling in love, birth houses into homes, birth revolutions,
birth open hearts, birth listening to our bodies

birth the god in you - without even touching you

So, want to do something revolutionary?
And fall in love in a time like this?

You Left Your Scent

Bossa Nova plays in the background
I am missing you again
by the way,
you left your scent
and pieces of your pain
that you'd hope to sink into me

but I kept my body to myself
not giving into flames of desire that would leave us
Ashes

Rather, let this flicker burn slowly
let me show you what the moments in between healing looks like, for
Moon never rushes sun to rise

always reflecting light
just to control high to low tides
sunsets walk longingly along the shore, a soft
desire to awaken, a heart that's been broken
as the horizon cracks open to invite starlight

Don't let this flicker
turn forest fire
that reflects the sun, for
moon never rushes sun to rise
moves only gracefully in the dark

just to love you slowly
show you what loving in between heartache looks like
I won't be your rays on sun filled days
Only reflect your light, like
Moonbeams at night

bossa nova slow dancing,
never rushes sun to rise
Loving your scent in every step
nose grazes your chest
eyes gazing for some seeing
as lips wait, burning
by the way

you left your scent
And pieces of you
aching for moonlight

It Could Have Been

I remember the moment my guarded heart opened for you
I won't tell you when and where
It could have been when you smiled at me at the cafe
over chilaquiles and green salsa
It could have been on the dance floor to salsa or bachata
It could have been in the morning light or at night
full moon delight

It could have been one of the many conversations
over the phone or in person
Your scent on my lips, your hair on my fingertips

That is when I fell for you
I know it is all a game to you
To reach out when you want
Take the energy that sustains your creativity
So I let you go
For I know when my heart aches for something more

I recognize when it's love
and when it's not

Future Home

I write to you from a far away place
Not a penny to my name but richer than any man I've ever lied with
rich like the ocean waves crashing on my golden skin
rich like when my eyes hold you like the warmth of the sun
rich like when we kissed and fire burned us into ashes

I write to you my future home where I land my feet on cobblestone
and rest my head on throws and pillows
A house, I will make a home
with a hacienda and hammock
and fountain where I can dip my feet and birds can come and drink
where laughter over chilled tequila is met with dancing
under full moons
silent conversations spoken from
cafecito eyes

I look out the window to watch our children play
and their children
I will see years go by as the foundation dries
to grow old with you and we will argue, make love, make up
in the home with cobblestones

Life Long Lover

Hurry up please
I know in this case, in these streets
I suppose I am learning patience
I am learning what to say to you when I first see you

Now this is not naive love
or the typa love that fantasizes
this is the love that builds

See all of you
Be a witness to your life
From the mundane, to the mistakes
to the all the victories

I write to you as if you are here
as if you are listening to my words
after a long day of work
We are both tired but in love

rest my head on your chest
Let the rainfall outside be our meditation
as we are cleansed from todays pains
Fingertips brush your face
let me love you back to life again

There's soup on the counter
I've been warming all day
The bath waits for you
Water to run you through
As I warm your neck with kisses

Before You Love Me

I've walked away a thousand times
Said no about a million more
And found myself
In unknown places - the
I can't believe I got here places

So I'll say no until I say yes
With someone who can walk next to me
Smell my hair, hold my hand and go to
'the I can't believe we got here type places'
The awe and wonder places
Leaving us breathless

From kissing too much
Loving too much
We might get lost a bit
If you don't mind
Down a windy road

But we'll find ourselves again because
From the beginning we knew love
But for ourselves or maybe tired to
Loving ourselves just enough, to love you
I won't waste my breath when I tell you
Before you love me,
Love you.

I Hope You Can Fly

If it was meant to be
Wouldn't it be so loud in my soul
That it would be like trying to holding back the ocean
But so quiet it would be like trying to hear the night sky
I can not deny what is not echoing
Inside me

The power of choosing someone
It weights of heavy with responsibility
If you don't mind
I have some more loving of me to do

I suppose it could be in practice with someone
but
Let me collect my thoughts
Gather up the feels I've buried deep within
being with me

If you are with me
Will you see and hold all sides of me?
Battling demons and monsters
As I turn them inside out, upside down
Thank you for the flowers and all but will you
Love me messy?

Or are you too sweet for that?
You have yet to unlayer your night skies
Have you entered that space to see what
You have in common with the stars?
Have you found the god in you that helped you
Accomplish this daring task
To walk through darkness just to realize

  you are the light

Because loving me is not just being a really good dater
Or talking nice
Have you thought of the value in your legacies?
Pride in majesty in the names I will carry?
Will you rise to the occasion as a protector, provider?

Will you let a woman challenge you, to your best self?
if not,
I hope you can fly while falling for me
Cuz I'm not gonna catch you

Never Abandon You

Everyday I get a little bit stronger
I gave so much of my energy to you
I am spent
But there's this one last spark in me
That I saved just for this moment

She's burning through
Making her way back
To the body that is my home
The fire is painful
But it's cleansing

I drop into myself again
And little by little I invite
The pain through
Feel to heal

It's okay, I say
You're allowed
Just don't swallow me whole
Know you'll be met with
Compassion, every step of the way

I promise
I will never abandon you

This is when I met my power, face to face

Chapter 4

wisdom

of

friendship

What Saves Lives?

I often think about if I am working in survivor mode
If I am too comfortable knowing I deserve more
My Tia says people who are delusional are often not ready to face reality

More often than not I am tapped out of reality
Exploring other realms of possibilities
Just to survive
To save my life
Tapped out or tapped in
It usually means I am dreaming
Dreaming of a better life

Dreams.
I told a date one time "I got dreams, what do you got?"
He said "A 401k"
We laughed

But he also said mundane
I say: I will get there one day
Knowing it is not far from reach

You can do a lot in one year
Mama said one foot in front of the other wins the race
One step out of bed
Look at the mirror not at your clothes you said you would fold
While you were reading your favorite book
Or writing your own

Just to stay alive
Just to say this life is worth living
Just to say I will make it to morning
while my dreams keep on living

Count your blessings
So I count the people who love me
Like unconditionally
The chosen family
You can tell your whole life to them but you don't
There is time to unlayer, because they not going anywhere

Next to dreams are the people who get you there
My fallen angels - flew out of heaven just to love me
Went through hell to find heaven together
Roses from concrete
Just their presence makes life worth living
Makes life worth dreaming
Keeps me believing

When My Bestie Dances

She knows how to walk into a room
head held high
chest widens with pride
space is made for her
as eyes wander to her fragrance and presence

When my bestie dances she smiles
Outshining any try - hard
To watch her is to feel again
light to the eyes
a prayer that liberates spirit

She turns and you turn on
bring all your offerings to her hips
Lay down your burdens to the dance floor
as she moves them, unearths them
unlayers them into her own melody

You forget why you hurt yet,
Feet ache for each beat and drum
her body poetry resembling the night sky

When my bestie dances
she breaks curses
as ancestors are shaken awake
"Look! She sees the god her." that

Outshine the rays of the sun
because she is moon mistress dressed in sweat
beads drip down to show her glitter
feel what she feels
as twists and turns
each step a new milky way
Lose yourself in the clave, the rumba and the
awe struck starlight of her

My Girls

when I am tired
they manifest for me
take my dreams envision them in the galaxy
Unearth my soul and inflame my spirit
They know the desires of my heart, my deepest secrets

when I am doubtful
they refuse to let it linger
they reach into my mind
and burn me with my own light

remember who you are

A Bad Bitch
Main Character
Warrior
Moon Mistress
Divina
Goddess
Lover girl

Force of Nature

A Woman

My girls are visionaries
Seekers and safe spaces for dreams
They carefully place in their hearts
All of me, the oceans and deserts and wild things

They see me as goddess
Council me into better, because I reflect them
Want the best for them
They love all sides of me so I can do the same thing
to embody all the dark and the light
Remind me they will still be here for me,
in every dream I reach

As they bring me back to earth or lift me to the skies
They know what to do
My girls hype me up when I feel pretty
when I feel ugly
they know someone will fall in love easily
because who wouldn't want to love the love that
loves me

She is perfectly imperfect
all the crazy and all the peace
the wholeness she carries
even with insecurities
Dancing to release what no longer serves us
Healing to take up more space,
Building empires with long lasting legacies
we work together you see

My sister, my mirror
how I love her is how I love me
She knows what works and what doesn't
to push me into my greatness
clouds turn to ray filled days

She the flower in the bed that stands tall besides me
not waiting to be picked but doing all the seasons with me
Bring pretty but also brilliant becomes less lonely
for she can see me eye to eye, up and down, side to side
World seems more mother earthly
I am nurtured again
from root to tip

loved by the greatest love anyone can have

the love of a woman

who happen to be
my best friends, my girls

Mariposa

My love, there are wings waiting for you
the air ready to hold you
as the fire has turned ash now
sweeps through your bones
There awaits deep within
answers that need emerging

They may not look the same as others
in fact they are made just for you
nor does your soul look like another
molded, crafted just to melody you into sound
into palms that calm and cleans every ache of you
to be your own healer

a gift we all embody

In the magic of presence
where we slow down to catch up with peace
Dust settles as we craves solace
Some spirit, some prayer that lingers a little longer
flicker finds ablaze again

I am awakened by my own light
that when muffled, shakes me open as
I kneel to the storm to pray and ask if I
wait for it's passing or become it

these are the moments that scare but excite me the most
when I know it is time to move forward
time to shed of myself again
it was so nice to soften my comfort in the shadows
but seeds watered like mine
are meant to break into the sun

I am ready to greet you again and awe of your outcome,
Don't worry if the wings will fit
For they are fit to fly
they are yours my love
made just for you, by you
to soar just beneath the moon, together with the stars

Chapter 5

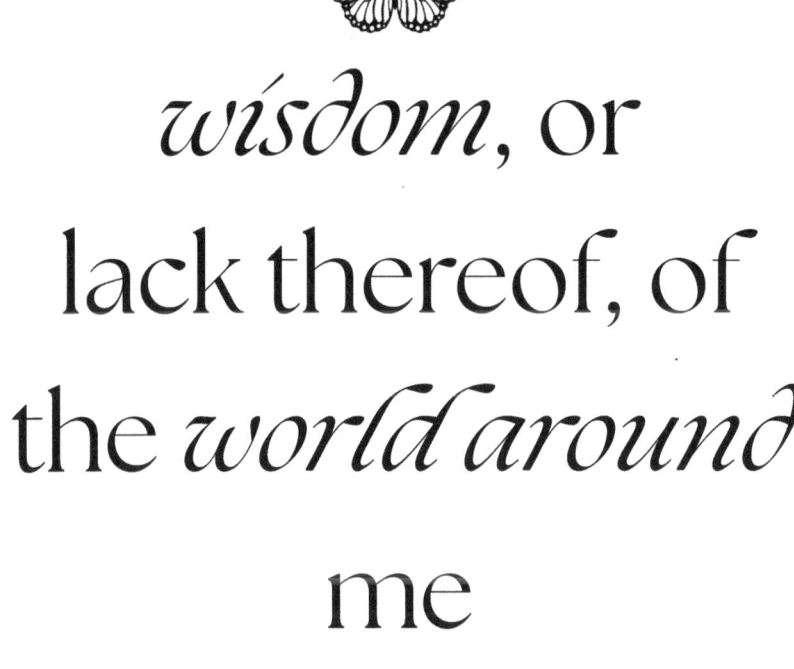

wisdom, or lack thereof, of the *world around* me

For the Maids

I've cleaned after people I never knew
I have learned about them
in what they leave behind
how they care for their environment
and I wonder

If they think of the woman who will pick up after them

I have been in the belly of the beast
I have seen the scariest monsters mistreat the kindest souls
And I've seen these kind souls suck at the nipple of these monsters not
knowing they have a choice
To be free
To know their value and worth

I've seen my people value work over sacrifice of their dreams
losing sight of what makes them truly feel free…
I understand survival mode
working until your eyes close
working to put food on the table
working for the purpose to survive
but may we live in a world where we have more than one choice
And that is in community not individuality …
Love and freedom through working to be free not less

How I've sat with maids and brown workers
who don't feel their own essence and ancestry
The victim mentality
the scarcity mindset
The "I need this job" when that job needs them

It's then that I realize I'm not on a hero's journey
I am in fact an artist.
To see the beauty in loss
in the darkest times
To see when injustice is being done

And to shed light on it …
To be a writer that tells the story of my people and of me
And to most importantly
Not get too comfortable
in the belly of the beast

For the Maids Pt. 2

Lucia misses her son
She wishes to see him
But the Senora does not allow the maids
To go outside her gated Beverly Hills mansion
on weekends

Once a week they get a day off
How freeing that must be
But not enough time to imagine or dream
Not enough time to rest or
To clean up their own homes or
see their own families

She sighs and all I can say is

"One day, you'll have so many days off"

One day.

Souls want my poems as they look

with curious eyes and hungry hearts

they need to hear what the universe has

for them

the sound of the typewriter

the breeze of the salty winds

gentle rays of the sun

there is so much more where

that came from

there in you – the answers form

where your body meets your

mind to find your heart

and where you are looking into

Free will

Free will is measured by opportunity
Free will is wether or not you were born into money
Free will is to stay inside or find where to hide
Free will to cook at home or eat scraps all alone
Free will everybody got a choice but we aren't taught that we deserve to
choose have the freedom to
Free will I got work to do but depression too
Free will what is free if your life is caught up with paying bills
Free will I am here to explore the world but internally
Free will to realize too much of anything isn't good
even freedom

Free will to understand that I am forever a student of life and love

Flames

I forgot that when you shine
Under pressure
Under water
Under pain

Others wonder
Others wonder why you don't shake
Why you don't crumble the same way
Why you don't run away

I forgot
That when ignited with fire
I start forest fires
I forgot that my flame

Is not seen the same way

Who does she think she is
What gave her the right
It was my pain and my strife
To be better on the inside

Calm rage met with
Smiles and a soft gaze
gentle words of praise
Rising from the ashes

You can not act the same way

You are no blank canvas
No need to reinvent, repurpose and reuse
You have gold in your veins
Your ancestors chains
Freed with glory to share this story

You are not seen the same way
Calm my flames
Learn from the pain
Pave the way to relearn again
Because

Your rage is not seen the same way

When the World Stopped

The world slowed down
Facing life in the same space
Routines in disarray
No distractions at play
But suddenly

The world stopped
For 8 minutes and 46 seconds
Hearts shattered
Minds shocked

It's 2020, and his name was George Floyd

The world began to unravel
Black blood bled red
Like how it always been, like how brown skin bleeds and sweats too
Are we human yet?
They called us radical
Rioters, angry, rebels
they hope that we forget
all we want is equal treatment
lucky we dont want vengeance

But we were lied to
Told if we did things peacefully
Stayed silent and listened
We would get recognition

So we tore down walls
Equality and justice isn't for all
We refused to ask for permission
Demanded a new institution

We called it a rebellion against
systematic oppression

The unrest
That rose with the spirit of our ancestors
into us when it was hard to breathe
When it hurt to just be

The unraveling has begun
weary, broken, tired
Yet we still carry on
Planting seeds that will unearth into new worlds

Dream worlds
The ones we're fighting for
With broken hearts that quickly repair themselves
For the next outcry

We hope to see that day
Making our ancestors proud and tell
Our grandchildren stories
Revealing our hearts about the
Pain and the glory

All I can ever hope for is a sparkle in their eye
That says 'thank you'
With minds and hearts that scream freedom

Bewildered

Is there a reason why
we sing the national anthem before every sports game?
we sing it to remind the other team who is also from here...
that they are also American?

In other countries this never happens
the only time it does is during the Olympics
To show country pride and remind the other team who they are up against
through song

America is like the embarrassing uncle
Who is always talking about that one time he did something semi decent
Trump as the golden poster American boy
Thank god for him..exposing it all
How the hell does he still get to run anyway?
Can I run?

America is not shy about showing off
And reminding us how truly behind we are
just embarrassing as the UK getting their next King
at the age of 75...
75 until life.
I guess the apple doesn't fall far from the tree
like Joe can barely stand

All these embarrassing uncles
tryna be cool
talk new, hide the mess
Which so clearly towers behind them

but we all know
they did some weird shit back then
you can see it in their eyes
In their smirk like they tryna offer you candy
get off me!

America you are second hand embarrassing
I mean you didn't even build your own streets
you have people who are not from here do all your hard, laborious work
underpaid or not paid at all

Call it freedom or just a scam

Brown Enough

Do I represent you enough
The first gen from East LA or the Dreamer who
Claimed this land long before lines were drawn
But I have been here 4 generations
to take the land back, to live out dreams the
Dreamers crave for their legacy
For our ancestors freedom

I was born the only one of me, 4th generation LA native Chicana
the first of many but the Spanish language I lack

But you see, I come from brown enough legacies
grandparents and parents who owned property and businesses
Legacies who were, teachers with masters
detectives, property managers, bankers, accountants
school principals, school psychologist, doctors,
playwrights, actors, musicians, mothers, warriors, artists and dreamers
what richness I come from

Aren't we enough?

So I create my own category of brown me
because I have privilege in my legacy
Carved out a place that carries the richness of my ancestry
something comforting about mariachi music and cumbia
something familiar about making tamales during christmas
something freeing about picking out words in Spanish to make it make
sense

See I was no blank canvas or Spanish speaking immigrant
I am the best kept secret of the empires, civilizations and tribes born within me
that remind me of my enoughness in my brown skin
generations before me set the table

As they conformed into America's delusional dreams
Freedom of Speech?
How their tongues were unaccepted, even in accents

Lost the language of the colonizers all together
Speak English like a settler, just to survive on beans and rice

But I am...
Brown Enough to speak truth to power, unapologetically
take up space where they tried to white us out
I come from brown enough masterpieces who remind me to never forget
my history, the land that was taken from me

Brown enough to gift me with feeling the pain they chose not to feel
What privilege it is to be a chosen one
Equipt with all the tools that will heal lineages before and after me

Brown enough to say we have adapted to fit in, to survive
to assimilate, protect our bold personalities, adopt what is accepted
but still not enough for one group
Despite similar pain we have gone through

So I will carve out a space for me and for those who come after me
We are enough, a bit more healed than the last
As we remember what no one can take away from us
Our Dream to rise from the land that once was ours

Together We Will Grow

I am fourth generation Mexican American
yet I am the best kept secret of the
great civilizations and empires
born within me

When I light a white candle
my ancestors whisper to me about their dreams
how they saw everything as sacred
For my ancestors did not take
we thanked - the gods everyday
Nor did we cast envy, but traded
Nor did we stand idly, but served

They say history is written
by the ones who win the war
but before brown skin bled red or lost breath
Stories were told about earth and sky
Our blood was made to create
prophets, creators, healers, warriors, and lovers

Before captivity my ancestors
Whispered prayers to the trees
Sang to the rivers
Cried from the mountain tops
Danced around fires

Now, Mother Nature tells me everything she remembers
She shows me the ancient secrets
of advanced systems from minds
far greater than the colonized

I am met with memories of
Nature nurturing civilizations
on land that was cared for
Land does not belong to us, we belong to the land
The ground reminding me
how my skin matches the soil and because of this,

gardens grow from my soul

Gardens that mariposas love to visit
For Mama told me to never chase butterflies
But if I slow down, walk patiently
Softly tend to the flores in their blossoming
Mariposas will always come to me

I was born prophet and goddess to a motherly saint
who dedicated her life to children and rosaries
A father who caught mamas eye in his mariachi suit
as his guitar met the melody of her laughter

My story is their story retold, rewritten, rewired
despite the pain
to start a revolution of brown rest
brown joy, brown love and brown legacy

I give you permission familia

To hold space to feel good
To imagine a sweeter life
To believe in your dreams that believe in you
To smile to the sky to dry your eyes
To let the sun love you and kiss your skin, till it is

the color of the earth
watered from our abuelitas eyes
together we will grow
with all our pain and all our love

To become one

with our land again
with ourselves again
with our lineage again
with our love again

About the Author

Monica Salazar is a Los Angeles Native and 4th generation Chicana. She is not only a spoken word poet. She is a curator, a facilitator of self love poetry workshops; a business owner and founder of typaway poetry, building her own niche and demand creating custom on the spot poems using a vintage typewriter. She's a networking chingonx and has collaborated with many businesses and nonprofit organizations throughout Los Angeles county based on her on demand poetry and workshops. She has been awarded by the United States House of Representatives with a Certificate of Recognition applauding her achievements as a business owner and artist in service of her beloved Los Angeles community. Monica Salazar is all about infusing healing power of the words for individuals in need of self empowerment, bringing individuals and communities in the forefront to be felt, seen, and heard. In her free time, she loves to dance salsa and Bachata, spend time with loved ones and friends and swim in the ocean.